Pebble™ Plus

Bugs, Bugs, Bugs!

Walkingsticks

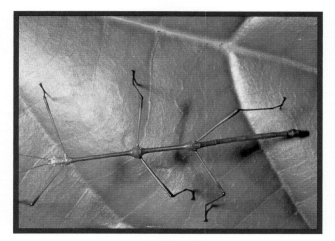

by Fran Howard

Consulting Editor: Gail Saunders-Smith, PhD
Consultant: Gary A. Dunn, MS, Director of Education
Young Entomologists' Society Inc.
Lansing, Michigan

Capstone

Pebble Plus is published by Capstone Press,
151 Good Counsel Drive, P.O. Box 669, Mankato, Minnesota 56002.
www.capstonepress.com

1 2 3 4 5 6 10 09 08 07 06 05

Library of Congress Cataloging-in-Publication Data
Howard, Fran, 1953–
    Walkingsticks/by Fran Howard.
    p. cm.—(Pebble plus: bugs, bugs, bugs!)
    Includes bibliographical references and index.
    ISBN 0-7368-3645-4 (hardcover)
    1. Stick insects—Juvenile literature. I. Title. II. Series.
QL509.5.H68 2005
595.7'29—dc22   2004011972

Summary: Simple text and photographs describe the physical characteristics of walkingsticks.

Editorial Credits
Sarah L. Schuette, editor; Linda Clavel, set designer; Kate Opseth, book designer; Kelly Garvin,
    photo researcher; Scott Thoms, photo editor

Photo Credits
Bruce Coleman Inc./David T. Overcash, 5; Donald Mammoser, 6–7; E. R. Degginger, 9; Michael Fogden, 10–11
Corel, 1
David Liebman/Dennis Sheridan, 17
Dwight R. Kuhn, 21
Image Ideas Inc., back cover (leaf)
ImageWest/Jeffrey M. Greene, 15
James P. Rowan, 13
McDonald Wildlife Photography/Joe McDonald, cover
Nature Picture Library/Pete Oxford, 18–19
Photodisc, back cover (walkingstick)

Note to Parents and Teachers

The Bugs, Bugs, Bugs! set supports national science standards related to the diversity of life and heredity. This book describes and illustrates walkingsticks. The images support early readers in understanding the text. The repetition of words and phrases helps early readers learn new words. This book also introduces early readers to subject-specific vocabulary words, which are defined in the Glossary section. Early readers may need assistance to read some words and to use the Table of Contents, Glossary, Read More, Internet Sites, and Index sections of the book.

Table of Contents

What Are Walkingsticks?

Walkingsticks are long,

thin insects.

How Walkingsticks Look

Walkingsticks look like
sticks that can walk.
Most walkingsticks are gray,
brown, or green.

Walkingsticks are about
as long as a child's hand.

Walkingsticks have six legs.

They walk very slowly.

Walkingsticks have

two antennas.

Walkingsticks use antennas

to feel and smell.

What Walkingsticks Do

Walkingsticks eat plants
and leaves.

Walkingsticks lay eggs
on plants.
Young walkingsticks hatch
after a few years.

Walkingsticks sway

in the wind

to hide from birds.

Birds eat walkingsticks.

Some walkingsticks hide

on plants.

They change color

to look like the plant.

Glossary

antenna—a feeler; insects use antennas to sense movement, to smell, and to listen to each other.

hatch—to break out of an egg

insect—a small animal with a hard outer shell, six legs, three body sections, and two antennas; most insects have wings.

sway—to move or swing from side to side

Read More

Frost, Helen. *Walkingsticks.* Insects. Mankato, Minn.: Pebble Books, 2001.

Harris, Monica. *Walking Stick.* Bug Books. Chicago: Heinemann Library, 2003.

Paige, Joy. *The Stick Insect: World's Longest Insect.* Record-breaking Animals. New York: PowerKids Press, 2002.

Internet Sites

FactHound offers a safe, fun way to find Internet sites related to this book. All of the sites on FactHound have been researched by our staff.

Here's how:

1. Visit *www.facthound.com*

2. Type in this special code **0736836454** for age-appropriate sites. Or enter a search word related to this book for a more general search.

3. Click on the **Fetch It** button.

FactHound will fetch the best sites for you!

Index

Word Count: 89
Grade: 1
Early-Intervention Level: 10